I0468565

Forex

A quick beginner's guide

By Richard Smiths

Table of Contents

Introduction

Many people are drawn to the prospect of Forex trading because they have heard about the leverage that can be employed, using a small amount of money to control a large amount of money, and therefore with the possibility of making money much faster than you could by simply investing in, say, stocks.

Financial markets are gaining increased popularity these days and where the currency market once held a small share, it is now taking the lead. This is due to excellent return on investment, being easy to understand and welcoming new traders into this kind of investment.

If you want to be a successful Forex trader and earn money as you trade, then you need to arm yourself with knowledge and information about trading strategies and how you can conquer a challenging market.

It is not easy to execute profitably orders or to compete with other traders. With the right knowledge though, you will find that you can manage.

This book will take you through all you need to know, starting with the basic that are used in Forex trading, and moving forward to how you should trade, everything you should know about a trading strategy and why you need to be disciplined. All this information comes together so that you have the best tools in place to ensure you make some money. This is an excellent eBook for beginners, as well as those who are looking to perfect their existing Forex trading skills.

If you think about it, it is obvious that more is lost by Forex traders than gained. Simply, every trade has two sides, or two parties to the transaction, each of whom thinks they are going to gain. What one wins, the other loses. And although you do not pay direct commissions for Forex transactions, there is a difference between the buying and selling prices, called the spread, which effectively takes a little out of each deal for the Forex broker. Therefore, traders as a whole finish worse off.

The statistics are actually a little worse than that would imply. It's estimated that more than 80% (some say 90%) of would be traders fail and have to give up.

Let's get started

© **Copyright 2016 by Richard Smiths - All rights reserved.**

This document is geared towards providing exact and reliable information in regards to the topic and issue covered. The publication is sold with the idea that the publisher is not required to render accounting, officially permitted, or otherwise, qualified services. If advice is necessary, legal or professional, a practiced individual in the profession should be ordered.

- From a Declaration of Principles which was accepted and approved equally by a Committee of the American Bar Association and a Committee of Publishers and Associations.

In no way is it legal to reproduce, duplicate, or transmit any part of this document in either electronic means or in printed format. Recording of this publication is strictly prohibited and any storage of this document is not allowed unless with written permission from the publisher. All rights reserved.

The information provided herein is stated to be truthful and consistent, in that any liability, in terms of inattention or otherwise, by any usage or abuse of any policies, processes, or directions contained within is the solitary and utter responsibility of the recipient reader. Under no circumstances will any legal responsibility or blame be held against the publisher for any reparation, damages, or monetary loss due to the information herein, either directly or indirectly.

Respective authors own all copyrights not held by the publisher.

The information herein is offered for informational purposes solely, and is universal as so. The presentation of the information is without contract or any type of guarantee assurance.

The trademarks that are used are without any consent, and the publication of the trademark is without permission or backing by the trademark owner. All trademarks and brands within this book are for clarifying purposes only and are the owned by the owners themselves, not affiliated with this document.

Chapter 1   What is forex?

Forex or foreign exchange market is a market in which different types of currencies are traded from all over the world. Traders in this market are in the form of buyers and sellers who are trading in desired currencies. These traders include larger financial institutions which are interested in trading currencies. Many large companies are also taking part in forex and trading currencies on a regular basis.

Banks are working as dealers and investing money to deal in currencies. Currency conversion is also a source of income for forex market. Many types of currencies are converted through forex and the difference in conversion is taken as profit by the market.

One type of currency is given in forex system in order to get another type of currency. In this manner the dealer are able to get the desired types of currency in order to deal in the local currency of the country in which they are willing to make investments.

Characters of forex market system

There are some characters of forex market system:

•   Forex has huge volume of trading with high liquidity

•   This market in dispersed geographically

•   Forex is working for 24 hours per day with two days off for weekends

•   This market has different types of exchange rates

•   Profit margins in the market are set low

- Special system in forex for profits of involved parties

Division of daily income of forex

Latest investigation and research on the daily income of forex market has shown different types of ways through which it is making money. Here is the division of sources of income of forex market through which this market is making trillions of dollars per day:

- Spot transactions

- Outright forwards

- Foreign exchange swaps

- Currency swaps

- Options and other types of products

History and advancements in forex market

Exchange of currencies is done from ancient times. In the past gold and silver were used as a standard in order to change one currency to another. Gold smiths and silver smiths were also taking money in the form of currency and changing it with the precious items like gold and silver. Different types of things were also traded and exchanged in order to get desired currency.

Many people were also charging some fees in order to exchange one currency with another and making money through fees and earning commissions in the ancient times. With the expansion of countries over many areas the need for exchange of currencies arose due to which different types of methods were tried in order to find the perfect mode for exchange of currencies.

Forex system was started before the time of world war one. People were not happy with the use of gold in exchange of currencies and there was a need to use some standard in order to set values of different currencies. In forex there is a set value of any currency which is traded for getting other currency. In past the system of forex started slowly but it gained popularity at a fast rate.

Many new centers of forex started and the business was a success. Pounds were used on a large scale in the past for holding the currencies. Holding power of countries was more for currencies as compared with gold due to which the value of gold in comparison for currencies was reduced. People preferred to use currencies as these could be used easily for getting desired items at the desired place.

After world war two a law was made in order to trade the currencies in the limit of 1% for the par of currencies. That value was set so that the exchange of currencies could be done easily. The rate was increased to 2% after some years. The introduction of computers gave a new area and expansion to forex market.

Now computers are used on a large scale in forex market in order to get instant and updated information about different types of currencies and their values. In the past the system was not accurate and the forex market was forced to close for some time period in order to regain the currencies and have some sort of stability.

Due to lack of stability in the past some dealers had a lot of money and some had no money at all. Then rules were made which are used now in forex market to make sure that the business could continue without interruption. 1973 is considered as an important year in the history of forex in which many important changes took place and rules were made and some of which are still used in the modern forex system.

After 1973 many more countries took part in forex and the circle was increased due to which many more currencies were involved and the business expanded on a large scale. Now international rules are used in the forex market to make sure that the dealers can participate safely. Many brokers and participants from all over the world are using advanced computerized systems in order to take part in forex on a regular basis.

Chapter 2   The basic of trading forex and some strategy

Forex is used on a large scale and there are many strategies in order to get success in this market. Different types of people are dealing through forex and they are using different types of strategies. Some strategies are high in demand and used on a large scale by many people as these are proven to get success. However there are some strategies which are only popular among some people and not used on a large scale.

Support and resistance levels

Forex is showing different types of charts to users for showing results of working and progress. It is important for all the participants in forex to have understanding of these charts. When the users are able to understand the charts then they can identify the support and resistance factors. These factors are clearly shown in charts for users to assist them in making decisions for getting or leaving currencies.

Fibonacci indicator

Fibonacci indicator is an important strategy in forex. This is helpful for study of charts on the basis of past and current trends. Predictions could be made with the help of Fibonacci indicator and important decisions about currencies could be made. The situation in the forex market is changing all the time and there are many ups and downs in the form of waves. With Fibonacci indicator strategy you are able to make reliable predictions about getting or leaving currencies for profits.

Multiple time frames

Time frames in forex are changing and it is good to check the charts about currencies before making investments. You can check time frames of your choice but it is good to have some balance. You can try the balance with the time frame of 15 minutes and a time frame of 30 minutes and a time frame of 5 hours to check the charts. This will give you reliable information on which to base your future decisions to trade in forex.

Scalping

This technique is used by many traders who are new in forex. This technique can give instant results and new comers in forex like to get instant results. It is important to do some research in order to get benefits through scalping strategy as lack of planning could lead to instant losses.

Horizontal levels

This strategy is important in forex. Charts are showing horizontal levels for currencies over time and these levels are going to change for different currencies. Dealers on forex must check these levels and use them for their benefits. Understanding of charts and levels is an important thing for working and getting success on forex.

Average directional index

This strategy is based on the strength of the market. Changing trends in forex are involved in this strategy and it is not dealing with the changing in charts. With changing trends the demand of currencies could be changed. This strategy is helpful for changing the demand of a particular trend which can lead to change in the demand of currencies.

Carry trade

This strategy is working well for those people who want to get benefits in future. This strategy is based on long term planning and making investments. Many businesses like to use this strategy and get benefits in coming time. You can have long term plans for getting benefits with your instant investment through this strategy.

Candlestick

This strategy is based on changes in the demand of currency over time. Past trends are important in forex and these could be checked with the help of candlestick strategy. Forex is showing many types of charts and those charts which are based on past trends and demand of currencies are helpful and candlestick charts are among them. You can check these charts and use this strategy to have your final decisions about dealing in any type of currency.

Head and shoulders

This strategy is also known as shampoo strategy. In this strategy the peak is checked in any currency and two other peaks were checked. This gives the presentation of a head and two shoulders. Mostly the peak value is like the head and the other two peaks are like the shoulders due to which this strategy has got its name of head and shoulder strategy in forex market.

Trend trading

This strategy is based on trends which are changing in the forex market. Many dealers are trying to follow the trend and making investments for getting benefits. Mostly the top and bottom trends are used in order to make trading decisions. Many factors are involved in setting of trends due to which this strategy needs to be used with proper planning.

Divergence

This is an important strategy in which many factors are checked in the forex market for making decisions. Right decisions at the right time are important in forex market and this strategy is helpful for making them. When many factors are checked in the forex market through divergence strategy then the chances of success are increased.

Trading news

News is important in the forex market. Big news from important countries is always changing game in the forex market. It is important to make investment decisions in forex on the basis of changing news from major countries. Many types of trends are developed on the basis of changing news from countries.

Chapter 3   How to control stop/loss

Stops are important in forex market and dealers must have knowledge about using stops. If a dealer is not able to understand the concept of stops in forex then it will lead to losses and problems in dealings. There are certain positions for entering in the forex market.

Like the entry positions there are many stop positions which are to be used. Many factors are affecting the selection of stop positions in forex which are to be understood by dealers. If a dealer is successful in forex then other dealers will follow him and use the strategies for starting and stopping as used by that dealer. The results are shown to all the dealers and they can follow the steps used by other dealers.

Situations in the forex market are changing with time and there is no set rule to get success. It is important to take good care of changing situations and adjust the strategy when needed. Forex is filled with risk and chance and those who are active and trying could get instant results in the form of success and profits.

Many types of trends are working in the forex market at a time and it is important to remain active to select the best trend which will convert to profits. Main thing in forex is to use risk management.

This type of management of risk is going to reduce the losses in case of wrong actions and increase the profits in case of right actions. Risk management in forex is important and it must be practiced. Different types of risks are also taken in forex in order to increase the chances of getting profits.

Importance of stops

Stops are important in forex as the future is not able to be predicted with complete surety. There is always risk in prediction of future time and forex is based on future time. Sudden changes in future could impact the dealings and market situations in forex which are not predicted.

Dealers have to take risk however it is good to use past working to predict future in order to have a good plan of action in the market. Research has proven that those dealers who are working in forex on the basis of plans are getting more success as compared with those who are playing without any plans.

Many traders like to use the common pairs of currency as these are giving more winnings. Money management is another important factor in forex. Without management of money the traders are not able to get benefits from winnings. Lack of money management leads to losses of two times and winnings of one time.

This is bad situation for traders and they have to make plans for money management. Stops and profits could be linked in forex. If a dealer is setting a profit at 50 pips then his loss will also be at 50 pips. This percentage could be adjusted by selection of the best position of stops which are used in forex for increasing the chances of benefits.

Static stops

Static stops are easy to set and these are based on a fixed value. The value is set by dealers and when that value is reached then the trade stops. This is used for controlling the loss factor. Dealers can have this type of stop in order to have controlled investment in the forex market to control the loss and profits.

Example

If a dealer is willing to have equal chance of profit then he can set a one to one ratio and have 50 pips profit for 50 pips loss. If a dealer is willing to have double chance then he can set a ratio of one to two. In this case the 50 pip stop will go with a 100 pip limit.

Indicators for static stop

Static stop can be set on the basis of indicators. Dealers can use indicators of their choice to set a stop. These indicators must be based on the situations of the forex market so that the trading could be based on some realistic data of the current situations in the market.

Example

Setting of stop limits to 50 pips or 100 pips is to be based on the current market situations. Market can be volatile or quiet and the limits of stops must be based on such situations. If the market is in quiet situation then, 50 pips is a big move. If the market is in volatile situation then, 50 pips is a small move.

Trailing stops

Many dealers are using trailing stops in forex. Trailing stops are giving more opportunities to dealers as compared with static stops however more plans and experience is needed to use these types of stops in forex market. Trailing stops are used for making adjustments by dealers when the situations are in their favor.

Dynamic trailing stops

These types of stops are adjusted by the dealer when the trade in the forex market is taking place. Adjustments in such stops are based on a single pip which is done by the dealer and adjustments are made to control the factors for getting benefits and reducing losses.

Fixed trailing stops

These types of stops are adjusted as the dealings in forex market are taking place. A set value is placed like for every 10 pips the stop is used by the dealer under these types of trailing stops.

Manually trailing stops

These types of stops are used by traders in order to stop the trade when they want. Traders like to have these types of stops in order to control the dealings in the forex market when the situations are in their favor.

Chapter 4   Psychology of trading

Forex is a complex market and there are many modes of trading in it. Different people are having different psychologies at different times and conditions in the forex market. It is important to make plans and have right psychology in the market for getting success. It is not confirmed that a business professional will be successful in forex and a beginner is not able to get success.

Forex is providing equal opportunities to all the dealers and some plans could lead to benefits to dealers. Different types of psychologies are taking place in forex market, which are leading to different types of actions.

Greed

Greed is a main psychology in forex market. Many dealers are taking part in forex due to greed. This psychology is asking for more and making the dealer to act faster. Greed in the forex market is not fulfilled and the dealer continues to try the luck for getting more profits.

Many types of wrong actions in forex are taken due to greed. Many dealers in the forex market are looking for instant benefits in the form of profits. Greed of many dealers is attracting them to forex so that they can invest money and get more money in return in the form of commissions and profits. Decisions based on greed are going to give losses in forex and also in the real world.

It is important to overcome this problem of greed with the help of planning. Proper plans in forex are helpful for getting benefits and remain safe from greed to increase chances of success.

Greed is working like a demon in forex market. If the actions are based on plans and analysis of past actions in forex then greed could be avoided. Successful dealers in forex are able to overcome greed and take actions on the basis of knowledge and analysis.

Fear

Fear is another psychology of trading in the forex market. Many actions in forex are controlled due to fear when there is lack of planning and knowledge about the current situations.

Fear is working like a hurdle in making right plans of investment in forex. It is opposite of greed as greed can increase the investment and taking risks but fear is reducing the investments and chances of getting profits. Dealer with fear in forex is not able to control the proceedings and checking the results. Such dealers are not able to invest when it is the best time of investment as they are afraid of the losses.

This results in increase of losses as time is lost and reduction in profits as investment is reduced. Timely decisions are important in forex and fear must be eliminated with the help of knowledge and control of emotions. It is good to work in a conservative manner so that fear could be avoided to get benefits from forex market.

Euphoria

Euphoria is a psychology in which the dealer is thinking that he is going to get benefits in all types of situations in the forex market. This type of thinking is leading to make many wrong decisions which are giving losses however the dealer is not willing to control the decisions as he is overconfident that he will get benefits through his actions in forex without any types of plans.

Euphoria is mainly found in those traders who have got some instant success in their start of the forex market. Experienced dealers in forex are aware of the fact that forex is not an easy place to make money and hardworking is required for getting success. New comers in forex are suffering from euphoria and they think that they can make easy money.

Some instant successes are adding to this problem and they start to take actions which results in losses in the long run. It is important to make plans and consider the losses which can occur at any time in forex market.

Panic

Panic is another psychology in forex. This is making the dealers afraid and they are not able to invest money due to some instant losses. Forex is giving losses to one dealer and profits to another dealer. With panic the dealer is thinking that the whole market is in loss and any investment will lead to loss.

Such thinking is not right as plans could give results of the deals which could give profits. If a trader is suffering from losses in forex market then it will lead to a panic situation. Panic will lead to the making of wrong decisions in forex. These wrong decisions will adversely affect the trading of the dealer and more losses will result.

Panic can be avoided with the help of planning. It is important to control the emotions and psychology in forex. A dealer who is successful now can be failure in some time as the conditions in the market are changing with time. Panic is natural for a failing dealer in forex but control of emotions and making reliable plans based on analysis and knowledge is important for changing the failures to successes.

Chapter 5 Advantage of trading forex

Different types of advantages and benefits are associated with the use of forex trading. Here are some of the advantages and benefits in some details which can be obtained by dealers in forex markets.

Volatility of market

Forex is a volatile market and there are many chances of getting success. Instant results could be obtained through forex and money could be increased with the help of proper plans. Losses are also fast and those who are not dealing properly could incur losses.

- Forex market is large in size and has high liquidity

- More than 4 trillion dollars are traded in forex market on a daily basis

- Valid contracts are used in forex trading

- Volatility in forex market is helpful for getting benefits from fluctuations with time

- Volatility is increasing risks and benefits for dealers in forex market

Liquidity and market hours

Forex is an active market and it is inviting all the countries on a regular basis. There are many large dealers in forex who are investing money and getting instant results. You can see huge profits and losses in forex for different types of dealers. The situations are changing with time and a loser can be a winner in forex market with proper planning.

- Forex is working on a daily basis with 5 days per week and 24 hours per day. Countries from all over the world are taking part in forex and there are many overlaps which lead to a lot of dealings

- Dealers must understand the correlation among activity in the market and liquidity for increasing profits

Low cost for traders

It is easy to enter in the forex market. Many people like to use forex as it is charging less money as compared with other types of markets. By entering in the forex market the dealers are able to start with some amount in order to get experience and learning of the system. With time the amount of investment could be increased for taking bigger risks and to have more profits.

- There is a difference between bid price and ask price in forex. This is called spread and it is cost for dealing with brokers in the market

•   Spreads in forex are economical and flexible due to which dealers can take part with less investment and less risks to take a good start

Trading based on margins

Forex is operated through different types of accounts. You can have your desired account through professionals and brokers in forex market. With the right account and proper plans you are able to make a lot of money in forex in a short time period.

- Forex can be used with the help of brokers who are working on the basis of margins

- Brokers can be used for opening accounts on the basis of margins and money can be deposited to start dealings. These accounts are different from accounts which are based on credits in forex

- Any type of dealing can be done with the help of a margin account. You must have margin in the account to continue using it for making investments in the forex market

- Margin accounts are supporting the use of leverage so that users can use more investments to have more profits in forex

•   Dealers like to use leverage through these accounts so that the amount of returns could be increased

•   Planning is required or the dealer can have instant losses in such types of accounts

Factors for getting profits

Different factors are working in the forex market through which profits could be obtained. Short sales are high in demand in the forex market and these could be used for increasing benefits.

If you are able to sell a currency at a high price as compared with the price you paid for getting the currency then you are able to make money and profits. You can also control the amount of losses by dealing in the short sales as these need some investment and give instant results. You have to remain focused and make timely decisions for making money in trading in the forex market.

• Pair of currency can be sold through short sale method without making investments.

• Short sales are high in demand and used by many dealers in forex.

• There is a difference among derivatives of currency. This difference could be profit or loss for the dealer.

•   Short selling is helpful for making money and earning profits even if the market is not working in a profitable manner.

•   Profits can be obtained by purchasing a currency with low value and then selling it when the value is increased.

•   If you sell a currency at high price as compared with the price you paid to get the currency then the difference is the profit margin.

Conclusion

Thank you again for downloading this book!

I hope this book was able to help you to know about Forex Trading.

Finally, if you enjoyed this book, then I'd like to ask you for a favor, would you be kind enough to leave a review for this book on Amazon? It'd be greatly appreciated!

Thank you and good luck!

Preview Of Day Trading a quick beginner guide

Chapter 1   What is Day trading

Day trading is defined as "the buying and selling of securities on the SAME day". It is usually done online and in hopes of taking advantage of and reaping benefits from small, short-term price fluctuations.

Here is an example: You could buy 1000 shares of Amazon stocks at 10:15 AM at let's say - $425 per share. 10 minutes later it rises to $426, you made $1 per share. Since you have bought 1000 shares, you just earned yourself $1000 in profit (minus a small commission for the brokerage). This potential to make that kind of money in such a short period of time is what attracts people to day trading. It is not uncommon to make $300 in 30 minutes, $600 in 20 minutes, or $1500 in 5 minutes, and so on.

it is not always this simple. I know plenty of people and websites are selling you the idea that you can get rich overnight by trading stocks. It's not necessarily impossible, but it's rather unrealistic.

However, you can make a lot of money if you possess certain tools and know special strategies. As with any profession, if you want success, you need a PLAN! Without a plan, you are wasting time, and even worse, you are wasting money.

I will try to show you all the mistakes you need to avoid, as well as some of my best strategies that can be useful. If you are determined and committed, I am convinced you can accomplish anything you put your mind on.

However, day trading is not for everyone. If you are not good at facing losses, I recommend you NOT to go into this field of business.

If you are interested you can buy on amazon. **Day trading by Richard Smiths.**

www.ingramcontent.com/pod-product-compliance
Lightning Source LLC
Chambersburg PA
CBHW070404190526
45169CB00003B/1101